Chillingham Castle
The Diary of an Amateur Ghost Hunter
Mark Fisher

For my wife Jemma,
The greatest person I have ever known.

"All houses in which men have lived and died are haunted houses. These harmless phantoms on their errands glide with feet that make no sound upon the floors"
Longfellow

Introduction

It was a mild February morning in 2000 when I first saw Chillingham Castle. I had only just turned fourteen. I received a phone call one morning from one of my friends who had some exciting news. "We are going to stay at a haunted castle!" said my friend, "and you're invited!"

I have always had a fascination with the paranormal and could regularly be seen engrossed in a book about ghosts or a horror story of some kind. The trip would be the perfect opportunity to experience something paranormal first hand.

I might see a headless horseman or a ghost walking the halls wearing clanking chains or maybe a knight holding his disembodied head under his arm in the bedroom....or maybe not. Maybe, I would experience something different, something real. Something that hasn't only appeared in the horror books of writers with great imaginations. Maybe I would experience an unsettling atmosphere that sends a shiver down your spine and makes the hairs stand up on the back of your neck, a sign that someone, or something might be there.
If you are expecting a story of phantoms with disembodied limbs and blood dripping corpses walking around, then this book is not for you.

This book is an account, a diary if you will, of my own experiences as a visitor to Chillingham Castle over the past twelve years. It will give you an insight into the history of a wonderful historic building that I believe is genuinely haunted. Haunted by entities that move about and communicate, and who have been a part of Chillingham for many years. I believe the spirits have the ability to make their presence known entirely to the visitor, but somehow clever enough to never leave any solid proof of existence behind...or do they? I will discuss some interesting tips on how to conduct paranormal investigations so that you may find evidence of their existence.

You will read about past vigils I have conducted, or been involved in, at the castle, and the strange phenomenon I have experienced, including electronic voice phenomenon (EVP), and interesting abnormalities captured on camera.

My experiences at Chillingham have forged my opinion forever about surviving personalities, and I am completely convinced that this castle is haunted and that spirits dwell here.

Whether you are a believer or not, read this book with an open mind and enjoy it!

History of Chillingham Castle

Chillingham began its existence as a 12th century defensive stronghold, building up from a fortified house up to the four towered fortress that exists today. It became a completed castle in 1344, when King Edward III gave permission to add battlements. The castle is steeped in local and national history, gaining fame throughout the world for its bloody past and, sometimes, shocking deeds. The family became titled after their contribution to bravery and command during days of early battles in the 1400s, and their honours survive in the family today with many ancient titles.

Chillingham's position was ideal for defence strategy during the border wars between the English and Scots. With spectacular views of the surrounding areas for miles, including the clear scope of the Cheviot Hills, the chances of an enemy creeping within a distance to attack by surprise were slim.

The secure, tall and solidly built watch-towers acted as intimidating, professional, deterrents to all who dared to challenge. It was an ideal stronghold where passing aristocracy and Royalty could rely on protection and the company of friends.
This ideal mixture made it an appealing visit for many personalities of high society at the time. King Henry III came to Chillingham in 1245 followed, in 1298, by the "Hammer of the Scots" King Edward I. In the 1600s Charles I, famous for his leadership of the Cavaliers during their battles with Oliver Cromwell's roundheads, stayed here for three very anxious nights. That was shortly before he was imprisoned, and later executed, at Whitehall in London, in January 1649.

King Edward VIII enjoyed his hunting expeditions at Chillingham, and many members of the Royal family have continued the tradition over the centuries and with several private visits to the Castle in recent years.

The castle has changed very little since the early days. The only significant structural change has been the addition of the Elizabethan long galleries which are slotted in between the towers. These include the galleries added between the two South towers at the rear of the castle, which include the castle's Library, Great Hall and New Dining Room. It was a change made to keep up with popular Tudor architecture and style and also in preparation for a visit by King James 1V of Scotland, when he came to claim the English crown.

Other than those changes to the castle itself, the 18th century saw the development of stunning and extravagant Italian gardens. These gardens were designed around marble garden urns given by the French King, Louis Philippe, who came to stay in 1832. The pattern of hedges was planned out, in 1828, by Windsor Castle's royal gardener, Sir Jeffrey Wyatville who was asked to create a magnificent and royal spectacle for Chillingham's own grounds. The famous herbaceous border, planted along the garden wall, is the longest in northern England. At the far end of the garden, the wide defensive wall is fifteen feet thick. This wall was used as a jousting "grandstand" in days of old and once extended entirely around the castle grounds.

The castle is still very much a medieval fortress, oozing with its original character of power, defence, sophistication and aristocracy. Anybody who has a desire to find a building in the world, virtually unchanged, and allowing a real glimpse of life through the eyes of a 12th century aristocrat or soldier, then this castle will, no doubt at all, provide the ideal experience.

Chillingham Wild White Cattle

When you thought that Chillingham could not possibly add any more fascinating facts to its long line of bloody feuds, affluent lifestyles, famous figures and ghostly goings on, you hear about the 'Wild White Cattle'. They are the one and only surviving herd of real wild cattle in the world. They are the remaining blood line and survivors of the once considerable population of cattle that lived in the many forests of England.

So fascinating is their history, and so pure is their species that pre-Christian pagans sacrificed them to their gods. These cattle were held in such high regard that they were thought of as 'sacred'.

The cattle were also useful during the border wars as they acted as a strong line of defence. The Wild Cattle were also a good source of food for hundreds of soldiers and the nobility who resided at the castle. They are, however, potentially very dangerous, so the public are advised not to approach these beasts alone and only under the supervision of the knowledgeable and experienced warden.

Family

Sir Edward Humphry Tyrell Wakefield, a Baronet, Lord of the Manor of Chillingham and owner of the Castle, was born on the 11 July 1936. He and his family live at Chillingham Castle when he is not travelling the world for adventure or lecturing to museums or factories to help the Castle survive the attacks of today's expense.

Sir Humphry purchased the Chillingham lands, but was gifted the Castle as it had never been sold in its thousand year history. The

Castle had been owned for hundreds of years by the family of his wife, Katharine, who comes from Northumberland's ancient and noble family, the Greys.

Katharine, the Hon. Lady Wakefield, is the daughter of Lord and Lady Howick of Howick Hall. Lady Howick was born Lady Mary Grey, and she would often visit Chillingham Castle throughout her long life. Lady Mary was born and raised at the beautiful Howick Hall, another great Grey property once a part of the Chillingham Estate. It was at Howick Hall that the Prime Minister, Earl Grey, first had the famous Earl Grey Tea mixed for him.

Sir Humphrey has spent decades restoring the once neglected ruins of Chillingham Castle to its present remarkable state. The Castle now houses the fascinating and varied collections he and his family have assembled over the generations, and the public can enjoy them all during the castle's open season.

Sir Humphry was educated at Gordonstoun School, which both Prince Philip and Prince Charles attended, and he has a Master of Arts degree from Cambridge University. He has made his career as a writer and traveller, but always with a professional study of antique furniture and historic restoration. He worked as an expert at Christie's of London and then became director of the most prestigious antiques firm in the world, Malletts of London and New York. In his younger days he served in many countries as a Captain in the 10th Royal Hussars. He is a life-long horseman, riding around the Chillingham hills on his horses, always bare-back which he loves.

Amongst his many national and international involvements Sir Humphry is most proud to be President of the Northumbrian Mountain Rescue Services and of Newcastle's prestigious Avison Ensemble. For a long time he was Chairman of the International Wilderness Foundation, he is a Fellow of New York's Morgan Library and of London's Royal Geographical Society. He was elected Honorary Life Member of the Harlequins Rugby Football Club and of the Cambridge Scott Polar Institute. For his Castle restoration projects he has, rightly, been called a "Worker of Miracles" by The Telegraph and "Legendary Restorer" by The Field

The Wakefield family has two sons and a daughter. Maximilian, the eldest son, inherits Chillingham and served in his father's regiment in the first Gulf war. He is a successful racing driver with a wife and young family. The younger son, Jack, is a writer and dealer in the Arts world. Daughter Mary, a musician and painter, is also the Deputy Editor of the 'Spectator' Magazine.

Reference: www.chillinghamcastle.com

Rooms and Alleged Hauntings

Pink Room

The Pink Room is one of Sir Humphrey's private apartments within the castle, only available to his family and personal guests. It is located high up in the north-west tower. Of the many eerie rooms in the castle, it is one that carries a story of great tragedy and mystery that occurred centuries ago and remained undiscovered until the restoration period of the late 1900's.

The story begins with a previous occupant of Chillingham known as Lady Leonora Tankerville. She was resident at Chillingham during the 1920's and was particularly fond of the Pink Room, most likely because of its magnificent views over the garden and interior. It was a room where she spent a great deal of time that is until the inexplicable began.

Late at night, the hauntings started. The tower clock would strike midnight, its chimes thudding through the castle walls. As the final stroke died away, an eerie silence would engulf the room. A silence that was so quiet and unnatural it would chill your bones to the marrow. Suddenly, the silence would be broken by the muffled cries of a child that grew louder and more disturbing with each cry. The shrieks and wails would become so unbearable that whoever was sleeping there at the time would be forced to block their ears for relief. The cries were often described as a child in agony or in great fear. After a while, the shrill cries would die away, leaving the occupant severely distressed, but the ordeal did not end there.

Next, a bright halo of light would emerge from the old fire place and slowly approach the old four poster bed. Within the calming blue light the figure of a young boy dressed in old blue clothing would appear. He would look at who ever was in the bed and gently stretch out his arm, as if wanting some form of comfort before vanishing as quickly as he had emerged. The occupant would be left shaken and terrified by the experience and would more than likely never return to the room again.

However, Lady Tankerville returned to the room each evening and witnessed the haunting on a regular basis, which was always repeated in the same manner and order, hoping to find what the ghost wanted. She hoped that he would speak and tell her how she could help him to rest or why he was bound to the room in spirit. He never did.
Leonora Tankerville kept a diary of the boy's visitations spanning over a long period, and then, during the restoration period, the reason for the hauntings was solved. The aristocrats who owned the castle at the

time decided to knock the wall down in the pink room to create a passage way that would connect directly to the next tower. Within the rubble, were the remains of a young boy and fragments of blue clothe. The clothing was identified as being from a time period when Charles I was on the throne, dating the boy's death to somewhere during the mid-1600's. His identity remains a mystery to this day and there are no records of any child living or working within the castle at this time.

The remains were given a Christian burial in the local churchyard and the haunting ceased, the ghost was never seen again...until recent years. Guests in the Pink room have reported being woken in the middle of the night by flashes of blue light near the fire place. It is suggested that this is caused by an electrical fault, however, there have never been any electrical works carried out in that particular wall of the room. Other guests have also reported that when they are looking in a certain mirror within the room a child's handprint appears before slowly fading away, leaving whoever is there at the time alone once more, with nothing more than an unnerving quiet and uneasy atmosphere about the room.

Library

The Library is a cosy and regal room with a magnificent fire place and impressive book case containing a fascinating collection of literature, spanning the whole length of the side wall adjacent to the windows that look over the back lawns. Generally a peaceful room during the day, it has moments of an oppressive atmosphere that comes and goes, mostly in the evenings. The hauntings generally happen when the room is occupied by one person whose mind is engrossed in their own business. It is said that the voices of two men can be heard talking. It is never possible to make out the gentleman's conversation, but the voices immediately cease when one stops reading or writing to investigate further. A mild haunting in comparison to other locations within the castle, but still very disturbing once the lone occupier realises that the conversation they tried to fathom is not of the living, but of past library sitters from years gone by.

Chapel

Like many rooms in Chillingham castle, the Chapel offers visitors an experience of individuality, uniqueness and beauty. A place of worship and peace, it still manages to omit a feeling of oppression and anxiety, causing many a visitor to exit the room at the earliest opportunity.

A traditional looking chapel containing an alter at the far end, a priest stand and a statue of Jesus Christ upon the cross on the far left wall.

The Library

The pews are set out in two rows facing the alter with an aisle that leads directly between the seats to the front of the chapel. There is one window directly above the alter, which looks directly out over the back lawns and fountain.

There are two entrances, one leading from the great hall, the other from the Minstrel's gallery.

The chapel is famous for its 'cold spot' which can be found right next to the priest stand. Even in the peak of summer or when the castles heating is on full power, the cold spot will remain. The room has been checked many times for explanations such as discrete draughts or a wind tunnel that may lead from an adjoining room. None have ever been found.

People have reported a feeling of dread when standing next to the priest stand, and even people who are unaware of the phenomenon speak of feeling the hairs standing upon the back of their neck and a feeling of anxiety. Imagine their shock when they are told of the paranormal activity which has been reported for centuries.

Another haunting associated with the Chapel is the story of 'Eleanor'. Eleanor has been sighted many times sitting in the pews, near the alter. She turns to look at visitors, face full of sorrow, and simply vanishes, leaving who ever sees her apparition in a state of shock. Eleanor is a young girl, roughly the age of 9. She is reported to have been a prisoner at the castle during the border wars between the English and the Scots. After days of ill treatment by soldiers, she was said to have crawled into the chapel, and died near the priest stand.

Her body was simply disposed of and nobody knows where her remains lie. Could they be behind a wall in the chapel or beneath the floor boards like so many other unfortunate beings from that time period?

The Chapel

Visitors have also reported hearing a child whisper in the chapel, and others have felt their clothes being tugged, as though it were a child seeking attention. Many visitors who claim to have medium-ship abilities, say they have seen Eleanor. She is a short girl, wearing a dirty white dress with mattered dark brown hair. Her complexion is pale and her expression a state of desperation. It seems, centuries later, that even her ghost still bears the memory of her neglect.

People have also reported the faint sighting of an old priest walking around the room. The Chapel is a fascinating and wonderful room to visit, but one may wish to reconsider entering it alone in the late evenings unless they did not mind the random apparitions of its inhabitants.

Great Hall

The Great Hall is a truly baronial room, and its interior remains unchanged since its early days. It was once used, and still is, for banquets and celebrations. There is an old dinner table that stretches almost the full length of the room, with the ability to seat many people. At the end of the room there is an ancient tapestry depicting a battle scene, most likely from a gruesome war that took place within close proximity of the castle. Opposite the banqueting table there is an old stone fire place that is colossal in stature, as it would have to be to fill such a room with heat.

There are many original artifacts in this room, ranging from ancient body armour to weapons of war, some of which would take ferocious strength to lift, giving you a mental image of a fierce barbarian who would have once decimated any man in his way on the local battle fields, using this weapon. Although the majority of weapons in this room have caused pain, suffering and death, there is one that carries an element of good and relief, if that can be believed. On the banqueting table is a strong piece of wood that has been reinforced with strips of steel along the sides. The 'weapon' forms the shape of a letter 'Y' and was indeed taken to battle but its use did not become apparent until the end of the battle. It is known as a 'priest stick' and a holy man would walk the battle field looking for injured soldiers who were beyond medical attention and were dying a slow painful death. The priest would simply mutter the Lord's Prayer and smash the club over the head of the injured until they were dead. The priest would then take a sword and make a small incision into the wood which would act as reminder to the priest of how many lives the stick had taken. They would then be prayed for at a later date.

The Great Hall

Many would assume that because the great hall is home to many weapons of such barbarity, then the room must be haunted. This assumption would be correct. Many people have reported hearing heavy footsteps echoing round the room when they have been standing just outside the door. On further investigation, there has been no sign of anybody in the room at that time. Another strange phenomenon is the moving of chairs. During a guided tour one evening, the group leader was explaining how a particular weapon would have been used, when suddenly, one of the chairs from the banqueting table at the far end of the room, closest to the chapel, scraped along the floor about two feet, before coming to a halt. Startled by the noise, the group turned round only to find the chair now standing in the middle of the room.

Another regular occurrence is the throwing of objects. Previous caretakers have often said that when they are locking up the Great Hall for the night, objects from the table such as cups, goblets and plates have been thrown and hit them on the back as they were about to leave the room. After turning around to catch the culprit, they were always met by an empty room with nobody there but themselves. Alone, with nothing more than an eerie silence for company. As you could probably imagine, they left the room a lot quicker from then on, or locked up in pairs! A common problem that many people encounter at Chillingham is the failure of electrical equipment such as cameras and video recorders. In most cases, the equipment will be fully charged when entering the castle, and within minutes, completely dead.

Many suggest that for a ghost to make a manifestation, they need a source of energy to draw from, therefore pulling all energy from the battery of an electrical appliance. So, if you ever hope to walk away from Chillingham with some nice photographs, may I suggest that you take two, or at least plenty of batteries! Cameras that are successful at Chillingham, or at least for a short while, often capture white balls of light.

These strange apparitions appear on cameras throughout the castle but more so in the Great Hall. These are commonly known as 'orbs' to the paranormal enthusiast and it is suggested that they are the early stages of a ghost's manifestation. If this is the case, then the great hall certainly offers refuge to many, as some photographs have been known to contain at least fifty!

King Edward I room

The Edward I Room is the most ancient Room in the castle. Aristocratic visitors and royalty would spend a great deal of time here. The location of the room was perfect for safety, high above the ground which could be potentially attacked, with fantastic views of the Cheviot Hills and gardens, a view fit for a king. It also acted as a good watch tower for any uninvited guests. The room is named after the visit of "Proud Edward, Hammer of the Scots" in 1298, on his way to the battle of Falkirk where he captured William Wallace, otherwise known as Brave Heart, who had invaded the previous year, burning women and children in the local church (situated just outside the castle's side gate).

King Henry III is also reputed to have stayed here in 1245 when he came for his planned sudden attacks on the scots. The magnificent gothic window overlooking the garden may have been designed by William of Durham who designed the Coronation Throne in Westminster Abbey which covered the famous Stone of Scone. Chillingham has many connections to famous architects and artists who have become known worldwide for their works throughout the country and beyond.

The Edward I Room has been restored in a way that represents its original standing from the 13th century. Its interior includes suits of armour, some weaponry and a banqueting table (similar to that of the great hall) and is set out in a way that echoes the castles vibrant past of those bloody feud days. Also on display is the castle's "License to Crenellate", which means permission granted by Royalty to build battlements, issued in 1344. This license was not given lightly, as it was originally a concern that it would make it a very difficult strong hold to attack, if the Royals felt the need to do so. The license was drawn up by Sir Humphry Wakefield's forebear, William de Wakefield, secretary to King Edward III. Throughout the whole country, this is the only 'License to Crenellate' actually in its castle of origin.

Edward I Room

In a secret compartment, to the right of the north window, which is a solid metal box embedded in the wall, 125 Elizabethan documents were discovered during renovation. Some of the documents are related to plans and objectives during the days of the Spanish

Armada, and others include information about the Royal succession of James VI of Scotland.

The fine gothic window was installed for the Royal visit in 1298 and is still very much intact to this day. Anybody standing near or looking out of it can get a glimpse of what our previous Royals and Lords will have seen centuries ago in times of great anxiety and war.

Visitors to this room report feelings of dread and despair. It is suggested that they are feeling emotions of the Royals and Lords of years gone by, who had concerns of the enemy breaking through the defence structure, or battles and wars that they were overseeing, beginning to crumble and go in the enemy's favour. It is not difficult to imagine these feelings, as in most cases, the loss of a battle or war meant the King or Queen in charge would face execution, as was the case for Charles I when he stayed here just days before his beheading outside of Whitehall in London. Could these feelings of distress be his own, possibly an echo from the past?

People have also reported hearing muffled conversations in this room which appear to develop into anger. Like the Library, it is not possible to make out what these men are saying, but we can assume that it may be aristocrats, giving the importance of the room at the time, discussing battle tactics or political affairs that are not working out, hence the raised voices. Nevertheless, this is a very spooky room, with a great deal of history and where many important decisions will have been made.

The Minstrels Hall

The Minstrels Hall has been a room of entertainment for the family for many years. It is connected to the Chapel by a passage way leading up some stone stairs.

Many years ago, the minstrels would congregate on the balcony and play music for the guests below, in what is now known as the tea rooms. It contains fascinating wooden chandeliers, old tapestries and the world's biggest elk horns. This particular room had a hidden secret up until recent years, where a sealed off torture chamber was found. The original entrance to this chamber is hidden behind a magnificent stone fireplace, adjacent to the window that looks over the courtyard. The Chamber is directly under the floors of the tea room, and to get to it, people would have to walk down a spiral stone staircase where the fireplace now is. Many believe that the fire place was built to conceal the entrance as there was no need for further use once the boarder wars had ended. Above it, is a fascinating plaque that depicts a scene from an old Greek myth with the moral of the story 'Nothing is as it seems'. This is a very clever gimmick, for whoever concealed the chamber may not have wanted its history entirely forgotten, therefore left a small clue as to what it once was. I guess we will never know....however, I experienced a very disturbing paranormal encounter in this very room, and it was many years later that I made the connection between the hidden history beneath the floor, and the blood chilling account that I will discuss later in this book.

The Minstrels Hall

But for now, people have experienced shadows on the balcony that slowly walk into the chapel before disappearing. One visitor claimed that he was admiring the interior of the room when suddenly he noticed a man resting against the balcony at the top of the room. The man was wearing what appeared to be a white Edwardian shirt with black riding boots. He stood, glaring at the visitor before turning around and walking up the stairs and into the chapel. The visitor noticed that something was very strange, especially when the man made no sound at all, not even when he was walking. Complete silence. The visitor summoned the courage to run across the tea room, up the stairs and into the chapel, where upon entering, the Edwardian man was nowhere to be seen.

The White Pantry Ghost

In what is called 'The Inner Pantry,' a frail figure in white still appears. The treasures were stored here and a guardsman was employed to sleep here and protect it.

Legend has it that one night, when the guardsman had settled down to sleep, he was awoken by a lady in white and she appeared to be very

17

ill and looked slightly disorientated. She asked for a cup of water and it seemed that she was struggling to stand upright and had to use the wall for balance. Thinking it was one of the Castle guests he turned to obey and began to fill a cup of water. Suddenly, he remembered he had locked himself in and put the key on his chain. It would have been impossible for any visitor to have entered without him knowing.

This same pale figure is seen today, and it is thought the longing for water, pale complexion and disorientation suggests poisoning.

The Ghost in the Chamber

Not all the ghosts are those we see. Some are merely felt as "Impalpable impressions on the air," as the poet Tennyson says. There is this sense of something unseen yet distinctly moving; it can be a chill, dark creeping sensation, or maybe just an oppressive atmosphere. This is generally the case for many of the castle bedrooms, although some are most certainly worse than others. What we need to remember is that many of these rooms are over 800 years old. They will have seen their fair share of feuding and violence, as well as happiness and joy. It is suggested that people emit emotions, and this energy can embed itself within the interiors of a room. Could these feelings and atmospheres that we experience be a reflection of what happened long ago?

The Dairy

The Dairy is situated in the newer part of the castle. Anybody staying there will witness the spectacular views of the nearby valley from the bedroom window.

It was originally the castles dairy, hence the name, and also housed the castle's maids in nearby bedrooms. It has been suggested that there was once a nursery in that part of the castle as many visitors have been awoken in the middle of the night by the shrill cries of a young baby. The cries go on for a short while before gently fading away, leaving the terrified visitor alone once more. A cosy and traditional apartment with interior that represents its past use, such as old milk urns and other dairy utensils used in days of old.

I have my own stories surrounding this room which I will discuss in a later chapter. It involves a very interesting photograph that I took ten years ago.

Caretakers Lodge

The caretaker's lodge is the private residence of the castle caretaker and has been for many years. Situated a little way from the castle, down the old gravel path leading to the church, it has had its fair share of paranormal activity. The previous occupant had many experiences, but one in particular will haunt him forever. It was late one night, the wind was blowing a gale outside and the rain was horrendously heavy. The caretaker was just about to retire to his bed for the night when he heard the old bell ring outside. He cautiously approached the front door and carefully opened it. Standing in the torrential rain was a woman wearing an old cloak, the hood obscuring most of her face. She slowly lifted up her right arm, and the caretaker noticed that she was holding a letter. Shocked by this unexpected visitor, the caretaker turned back into the porch to find the light switch for the outside lamp. He hoped that he would get a better look at the eerie figure standing in the shadows. When he turned back to the door, the women had vanished. All he could see and hear was the rain crashing down, and the wind howling through the trees. The caretaker very quickly closed the door and locked himself in for the night. This incident took place several years ago, but current residents are still woken in the night by phantom knocks at the front door and the sounds of an old door bell ringing.

The Caretakers Lodge

The Still Room

Here you will find the curious witch who curses those who steal from Chillingham - and some of the letters from those who thought that it was a joke! Her portrait hangs above an old cabinet in the room. Nobody knows much about her other than she was a witch whose native country was Spain.

On the cabinet shelves are letters from people who have befallen her curse. The letters detail how illness and bad luck have submerged their lives and those who are close to them. Accompanying the letters on the cabinet are the returned stolen objects. These range from door knobs to cutlery. People have also been known to experience misfortune for only taking complimentary bath soap...and I was one of them! It was the day of my 19th birthday and I had been staying in the Grey apartment with my mother, brother and a friend. (This apartment plays a big part in the chapter 'my own experiences'). We were just about to leave the castle and turn in the keys, not before I had packed some complimentary bath soaps into my bag as a souvenir. My mother had parked her car at the front of the castle ready for us to leave and I noticed that I had her car keys in my pocket. I had recently passed my driving test and we all agreed that a pleasant drive out of the grounds was in order, with me at the wheel! So we packed the car, including the baths soaps and began to drive. All was running smoothly, that was until the clutch cable decided to snap at the end of the drive. The car got caught in a ditch and we had to use all our might to pull it out, with no success.

Fortunately, some workers from the castle came to our rescue, and were even kind enough to solder the cable together as a temporary solution to get us home. While this was happening, I very quickly took the soaps out my bag and returned them to the apartment. Maybe a coincidence, but I certainly did not want to take that chance, and I must say, I will never take anything away from Chillingham again. And I don't think you should either!

The Spanish witch portrait is very old and is engulfed in an ancient, thick wooden frame. Even the most skeptical person would not be able to deny that there is something very unsettling about it. Maybe it is the colours and shading that the artist has used, but I beg to differ! There is something odd about her expression. It is almost like the painting is alive...

Grey Room

The Grey room is a magnificent apartment that can be enjoyed by the public for overnight stays. It has two bedrooms that both lead out into a passageway that connects to a fine Elizabethan long gallery.

One of the most famous hauntings associated with this apartment is with yet another old painting, the portrait of Lady Mary Berkley, a former resident of Chillingham castle. She was the wife of Lord Grey of Wark and Chillingham. Lady Berkley was left alone in the castle for many years with only her baby daughter as her only companion after her husband had an affair and left her for her sister. The portrait hangs in the long gallery and once belonged to the castle nursery a few centuries ago, before being moved to the Grey.

Legend has it that she would step out of her painting and walk around the nursery. The children and nurses would be terrified by her appearance and would leave the nursery at once. People have claimed to see Lady Berkley leave her portrait while it has been in the apartment, but it seems to be a far less frequent phenomenon than it was in the nursery, however, people have reported hearing a women sobbing in the dead of night in the long gallery. Maybe she is more settled in the Grey apartment as this is where she wanted to be all along? Maybe she wanted her picture moved from the nursery for personal reasons? Maybe the nursery holds too many unpleasant memories of her husband leaving her and their baby? Whatever the case, the portrait is beautiful and has stood the test of time for many years. Although slightly faded, it has been the source of documented hauntings and eye witness accounts for many years.

The Grey

The Monk's trail

The Monk's trail is situated deep among the ancient oak trees directly between the castle's main entrance and the caretaker's lodge. It was originally the setting of a monastery, and all that remains now is a stone arch which was said to have been one of its doorways.

Much despair and suffering are connected with this part of the castles grounds, mixed with an element of good. The residing Monk's disagreed with the barbarity and torture that was inflicted upon the unfortunate souls who were banished to Chillingham and would intervene where possible by cutting down newly hung prisoners from the trees before they had met their gruesome end. They would also rescue others from the surrounding trees, who were hung in such a way that they experienced the most unbearable and painful stress positions that anybody could imagine.

The Archway of the Monk's Trail.

Unfortunately for the interfering Monks and condemned prisoners, their regular rescue plots were sabotaged one evening by a soldier who was on night duty. The Monks were sentenced to horrific torture within the castle's torture chambers, followed by execution of hanging from the very trees in which they used to walk and pray, but the hanging would never be clean and dignified. They were made to stand under the tree of which they would meet their untimely death and put the hanging noose around their own necks. They were then hoisted up off the ground until they were suspended in mid-air. It was at this point that they would be left to choke to death after they could no longer hold their body weight when grabbing onto the rope above them.

There have been many reports of apparitions within that area. Visitors claim to occasionally catch a glimpse of hooded men, who wander around the trees slowly with a look of despair and desperation etched upon their faces. Could these sightings be the spirits of the holy men who, upon trying to offer relief and mercy to suffering souls, met such an unforgivable and sickening end?

John Sage

Not all spirits that lurk the halls of Chillingham are that of the innocent who have perished there. Entombed within its walls are the demonic souls of people who, it is said, were genetically made from the fabric of the Devil himself. One such wretched entity is believed to be the spirit of former Lieutenant, John Sage who became known as 'dragfoot'. During his active years as a soldier, his leg was injured by a spear which severed the tendons in his lower leg during a gruesome battle with the Scottish rebels. After the injury, John Sage's services were no longer required in the field as he no longer had the strength and pace that once served him so well when fighting. His injury had caused him a great deal of pain and eventually became a permanent disability. In need of a substantial living, he was proud to be transferred to Chillingham Castle where he took on the role of head torturer, which was granted by the castle owner Edward Longshanks (1200 AD).

John Sage was a horrific man who lusted over the suffering and misery of others, particularly anybody of Scottish heritage. So resentful of his injury given by the Scots, that he vowed to invent torture devices that would cause as much pain as possible, designed to make the victim suffer for a lengthy period of time before entering death. His evil work would give him gratification for many years, where it was estimated that he would torture at least 50 of his Scottish enemies a week.

Sage loved nothing more than to watch the castle dungeons fill up on a daily basis with Scottish rebels, and he enjoyed emptying them even more. Prisoners would watch in horror as their cell mates were dragged out in chains to the torture chamber below. They would sit, in a foetal position, listening to the unbearable screams from the depths below, knowing that they would be next. The screams would echo through the castle's dungeons for hours before coming to an end. Waiting prisoners often tried to kill themselves before meeting John Sage in the torture chamber below by repeatedly crashing their heads off the stone walls within their cells. After all, that would be a merciful death compared to what awaited them in the pits below.

Those who were successful in this brutal suicide were lucky in their escape. Those who were unsuccessful were about to enter hell...

Although successful in his job, his enthusiasm inevitably brought his twisted career and life to a bitter end. One evening, his lover, Elizabeth Charlton, came to visit just as he was locking up the dungeons for the evening. It was at this point that the couple became heavily involved with each other sexually, and decided to participate in gross acts of debauchery within the torture chamber itself. During their bizarre and unhealthy act, Sage decided to place Elizabeth on one of his favourite torture devices – 'the rack'. Sage, uncontrollably, began to strangle Elizabeth during their height of sexual pleasure, and before he regained what little sanity he had to begin with, she was dead like so many of his victims within that room.

Unfortunately for Sage, Elizabeth's father (a Border Reiver, clan leader and outlaw), had gathered intelligence of how his daughter really died, after he had so desperately tried to cover it up. He ordered that Sage be put to an extremely painful death otherwise he would join in an allied attack on the castle with the Scots. Longshanks, who was struggling financially at the time and could not provide the resources to fight back against Elizabeth's father, agreed to the order. John Sage was brutally hanged in the grounds of the castle on 'Devil's Mile', otherwise known as 'Devil's walk' before a crowd of blood thirsty locals. He had a noose put round his neck, and was hoisted above the ground where he began to choke to death.

As Sage's body still twitched with life, his face purple and blue with his eyes bulging out of their sockets, the crowd began to slice and hack pieces from his body, including his nose, toes, and testicles, before he eventually became lifeless, suspended and swinging from the rope above, dripping with blood.

It is reported that John Sage's spirit is very active within the walls of Chillingham. Many have reported seeing the apparition of a tall, strongly built man, with a jet black beard walking around the castle's many rooms. There are no existing portraits of Sage, so it is very difficult to know if the spirit that people are witnessing, is in fact the dark soul of John Sage, but the biggest clue that it may be his wretched spirit, is that he can be seen walking with a heavy limp, and the sounds of a footstep followed by a long scrape along a stone floor can be heard echoing through the halls at night...

Extracts from recent visitors in Chillingham's Haunted rooms...

In all guest apartments, there is a diary for people to document their stay and share their experiences. Here is a specific entry from a guest some years ago. This is one of many, many accounts. Almost everybody has some form of paranormal experience to record when they come to stay.

"I felt this hand on my arm. It was a most friendly feeling, and I believe someone was trying to guide me to see something". "My camera just would not take a picture of the orbs and lighting I actually saw. Yet, when I developed my film, there were just those same orbs, but in different places and rooms, literally all over the place". "The guide told me not to be frightened, and funnily I was quite happy even with the distinct whispering I heard in the King Edward Room". "I did not expect to find anything of interest, but was completely charmed rather than frightened". "It was at midnight when Ralph woke me. I saw nothing but he...". "It must have been the very early morning. I thought it was my wife, and suddenly realised that I had come along alone..." And so on!

Lady Tankerville's Encounters

Lady Tankerville had enthusiasm for the paranormal. Below are passages taken from her personal diary regarding her other experiences at Chillingham castle.

LEONORA, Lady Tankerville, (Tankerville is an old 1400s Grey family title) lived at Chillingham Castle in the 1920's. She tells many haunted tales of her life at Chillingham Castle:

A "Precognition"

"The first time I ever saw Chillingham Castle was actually in the company of a ghost!
"I was abroad in France one early morning, asleep. Suddenly, I dreamed I was walking through what I now know is the Chillingham West Lodge entrance, and then proceeding along the avenue towards the Castle. I had never even heard of Chillingham at that time.
"In fact, I had made the acquaintance of my future husband some months before, but had no expectation of ever seeing him again. I knew nothing of his home and no one had described it to me, nor had I seen photographs elsewhere.
Finding myself there I was full of interest and curiosity, especially wondering why the Castle, if it was to be a Castle, was not visible from the end of the avenue. I later found this to be the case. Although

asleep, I remember asking myself what this meant, and wondering if I should ever see this Castle in the flesh. Then, suddenly, a young man came forward, introducing himself as my recent friend's brother. He said, "I have come to walk with you until my brother George is ready." We turned and walked towards the park and then my future husband joined us. The brother then disappeared.

"In fact this brother had sadly died in Afghanistan fully two years before, but I had no difficulty in recognising him later from a photograph. Maybe he was dissatisfied to leave his old home without the fulfilment of seeing his surviving brother married and settled. I never saw him again, but I felt his mind was now at rest."

The Dying Officer

"Those who have just left their bodies are so often seen by their friends that the recital of such an occurrence becomes a mere commonplace today.

"Only last spring such a ghost visited me. – He was a young officer who we knew to be seriously ill but never thought of his being at death's door. It was after midnight and I stood at the dressing-table brushing my hair, with most of my clothes lying on the sofa near at hand. Suddenly, I became acutely conscious of this young officer's presence, and of being curiously scrutinised, and it was as if he were about to speak. Before listening or even looking, my first impulse was to seize my dressing-gown and throw it over me. Then, turning back, ready to hear what he had to say, he was suddenly gone. The room was empty and I stood alone.

"I told my husband that our young friend must be dead, and we heard next day that he had died at that very hour.

Ghosts of War

"The third type of ghost, where the figures moved as on films, appeared to me just before the Great War, when there was much occult disturbance of every kind in all countries.

"One morning, after an exceptionally busy time, I sat down for a few moments rest in a handsome room in the Castle overlooking the Cheviot Hills. The wind made sounds in the wide old chimney just like the distant boom of cannon. As I looked out on the restful formal garden, suddenly the waving branches and heavily drifting clouds assumed a menacing and warlike aspect.

"As I looked out at this wild scene, the form of a woman seemed to take shape before me, walking on the parapet of a tower apparently as solid as the one I sat in. She was in the garb of a Dominican Abbess. After looking eagerly towards the hills of Scotland, she knelt beside the battlements as if in prayer. A man stood beside her proudly upright, handsome and-richly dressed. He too was scanning the horizon toward the enemy country of Scotland.

"A few paces behind were two men in velvet court dress of the time of King Henry VIII. They were talking in subdued tones. In the background, on the further parapet, a halberdier paced up and down on sentry duty. I got up to watch the scene from the window, thinking I was about to witness some tragedy of former times.

"Presently I called to my son in the next room, but he was out. Then a housemaid came in to close the shutters and asked a couple of questions. I thought surely the vision would have disappeared. But no! Another woman brought the Abbess an ermine cape, and now the man's rich dress was covered by a surcoat. The atmosphere was tense with a feeling and sense of impending danger!

"I spoke to them twice, and asked if I could be of any service. When the man, who was now pacing back and forth, stopped and looked at me, it was the face of my husband. But he was in the garb of France four centuries ago! Then who was the Abbess? Was that myself? And why the anxiety? What was about to happen? If it was I, what was I praying God to avert? It was not long before we knew, and the din of battle sounded in our twentieth century ears. Shortly official directions were sent to us for action in the case of an invasion!

"I believe I had, quite inadvertently, 'tuned in' to a similar moment from long ago.

Blessed Skeletons

 Just below the floor boards of my writing room, estate workers discovered two grinning skeletons! They were lying against great, gothic carved stones, hidden to us till then. The real mystery to me is that I always sense the occult, a strong gift I have, which is why I have been 'sent' to Chillingham. Yet, I sense nothing here. Nothing, all these years with my writing bureau scarcely two feet above these puzzling bones. Nothing! Not even as I gazed at those solemn restful features.

NOTE: It was nearly a century later that we discovered that these bones lay in the ancient Chapel. So they would have received the traditional burial encouraging the heavenwards journey!

Conclusion

Why we do not all of us see these invisible things? I believe there is no inherent reason, as we all possess the same senses. We just need some understanding of those senses, and of the discipline to put it all to use. The ghosts of Chillingham, as with a radio set, have helped to show me we have the choice, for instance, as to whether we tune in to deep depression -- to the horror against which we are powerless to fight-- or rise up to the fairest heights of which man is capable and join and fight?

Chillingham Castle, LEONORA TANKERVILLE, (1925)

Reference: www.chillinghamcastle.com

Personal Experiences

People come to Chillingham for a variety of reasons and there is something there for everyone. It may be a love for ancient architecture, an interest in antiques or a desire to see fine Nobel gardens and woodland.

There is, however, something else to be found at Chillingham. It lurks in every room and hallway. It can be felt in the atmosphere all around. Sometimes, it may be nothing more than a sudden frosty chill that makes the hairs stand up on the back of your neck, disappearing as quickly as it arrived, although it can often be a feeling of great oppression, anxiety and fear. Sometimes those feelings can become so intense that many people choose to leave the castle all together in order to escape it. Even the most confident skeptic has been forced to admit there is something slightly unnerving about Chillingham. They may not be too quick to admit that it is the doing of restless spirits, but given the opportunity to find out, they in most instances, decline. And who can blame them? The thought of seeing the apparition of an ex resident sitting in the library, or hearing the cries of a tortured soul pounding through the halls at night can be too much to handle. But for the curious and brave who are willing to hunt for whatever lurks there, they will be sure to find it.

I have been a visitor to Chillingham for many years. On almost every occasion, I have experienced what I believe to be paranormal activity. I would most likely need another book to document my experiences as there have been so many, which is why I have made the decision to discuss the experiences I believe will have the biggest impact on you and which I have found most terrifying.

An Uninvited Visitor

In the bleak December of 2001 I spent the night at the castle in the Grey apartment. It was my sixteenth birthday, and I was accompanied by my mother, brother and two friends. The castle's atmosphere throughout the day was, surprisingly, calm and tranquil. We enjoyed walks to the lake and around the woodland despite the overcast, cold and dreary weather.

It wasn't until late evening, around 6pm when we were settling down for dinner, when a noticeable change began to occur in the atmosphere of the apartment. The staff had departed for the night and darkness had fallen quickly outside. We realised that we were alone, which was unnerving, giving the castle's reputation. The apartment seemed quieter, and every sound appeared to be amplified. There was a feeling of oppression which appeared to affect everyone sat at the table. We all felt scared but could not quite explain what we were scared of. It almost seemed as if there was a presence moving about the apartment that was malevolent. Who or what the presence may have been was a mystery at that point, but we were to have a rough idea later on that night.

Around 11pm we settled down to bed. My brother, two friends and I were sleeping in the bedroom at the end of the hall, which is accessed by three steps leading to the bedroom door. My mother was sleeping in the next bedroom, which overlooked the front of the castle. The door to the apartment was locked, making it impossible for anybody to enter without us hearing them, as it creaked loudly. For the next half an hour or so, we lay there trying to ignore the eerie silence which engulfed us, and that feeling of anxiety that had plagued our apartment since dinner.

Through the darkness of the room I could make out my friends and brother, wrapped up tightly in their blankets on their camp beds, eyes wide open, as were mine, unable to sleep. On questioning if everybody was fine, they surprisingly stated that their feelings of anxiety had heightened, and they felt sure that something strange was going to happen very soon. I too, felt exactly the same. Our prediction was to be correct and profound.

As we dosed in our beds, we were abruptly awoken by a series of knocking sounds. They appeared to be coming from the Elizabethan long gallery, which is the living room of the apartment. It sounded as though somebody, or something, was rapping on the old table that stands there. We froze as we listened, terrified. The sounds grew louder and louder, pounding and echoing around the gallery. What happened next was truly terrifying. The pounding stopped suddenly, plunging us into total silence, a silence so intense I developed a mental image of this entity standing alone next to the old oak table in the gallery, in the darkness, peering down the hallway that leads to our bedroom door, waiting to see if it had induced a reaction from us.

After a minute or so of lying there, frozen with fear, the pounding started again, louder and quicker than before. The terrifying sounds moved slowly from the gallery and into the hallway, pounding and thumping as though somebody was wearing big heavy boots, stamping away on the stone floor. As the noisy spirit drew closer, the sounds were so loud the bedroom floor seemed to vibrate, and the door frame shook violently. We jumped out of bed, fearing that something was about to burst through the door at any moment. It sounded as though whatever was in the apartment with us, was hammering on the bedroom door with a cannonball.

Just as we grouped together, clutching at each other's clothes like a terrified child, we heard my mother shout from the next room, "Can you hear that?"

"Yes" I shouted!

"What on earth is it?"

"I'm not sure, and I don't really want to find out!" I cried

"Stay where you are for now!" she screamed. No sooner had my mother finished her sentence, the pounding stopped and silence engulfed us once more, leaving us shaking and speechless.

Eyes fixed on the bedroom door; we listened intently, wondering what would happen next and suddenly, the silence was broken once more by the sound of a child laughing. It was almost like an echo. And then, it was as though whatever was there, simply turned around, satisfied at our fearful reaction, pounded and thumped all the way back up to the gallery, slamming the entry door behind it as it left. We jolted at the crashing sound the door made as it closed and almost instantly, the atmosphere lifted, leaving us feeling calm, but exhausted.

After checking that my mother was ok, although she was slightly shaken, as we all were, we decided that getting to sleep would be the best option. This of course was not to be the case.

Not as terrifying as our previous experience, but nevertheless frightening, we were kept wide awake most of the night by what sounded like furniture being dragged about upstairs in the apartment above, along with the familiar sounds of pounding and thudding. It seemed as though our recent visitor had retired to the apartment directly above us, known as the Lookout. We would have been more frightened at the time, but there was always the hope that the noises from the apartment above were being created by some restless guests, who had also decided to brave a night at the castle.

It wasn't until the next day, during our departure, when it was confirmed by the caretaker that nobody had been staying in the Lookout apartment that night. It had been locked for a few days, as no guests were due to stay there until the end of the week. Apparently, not a soul had entered that apartment that night.....

An interesting point about that night you may like to know is that while our supernatural experience was taking place, one of my friends had set up his video camera on a chest of drawers in the long gallery. The position had allowed the camera full view of the gallery, ensuring that if anything was in the room, we would surely have caught it on camera, along with any noises it may have made. On reviewing the footage a few days later, we noticed the camera had been turned off at the exact point the noises began, and resumed filming the instant the phenomena had ended. We could work out the time gap in the footage was roughly twenty minutes, switching off at 11.10pm and resuming filming again at 11.30pm, the exact time we experienced the activity. Whatever visited us that night clearly did not want any evidence left behind.

The experience had left us shaken, but convinced that something very odd was happening at Chillingham, in the supernatural sense. It had been too much for one of our friends, who never returned to the castle again. As for the rest of us, plenty more scares were in store, as we were to find out eight months later, in August 2002, quite possibly the most frightening experience of my life.

The Séance

A friend of my mother owned a health club in North East. She decided to raise money for charity, and consulted her colleagues for ideas. One colleague, a paranormal enthusiast, suggested a sponsored ghost hunt at Chillingham. He had investigated many reputed haunted houses before, and thought the idea of a sponsored trip would be exciting for the staff that worked there and would be a fun and unique way of raising money for the club. Once agreed, a team was assembled consisting of work colleagues, my mother, brother, one of my friends from the previous trip, plus another, who had never been before, but had heard of previous stories and wanted to experience it first-hand. She was in for an experience that she would never forget. We set off at 10pm. There were four cars required as there were twenty people to take part in the investigation. We arrived at the castle at 11.30pm where we were met by the caretaker, who escorted us to the Minstrels hall. I mentioned earlier in the book that this room would bare significance to a connection I made between the following blood chilling account that you are about to read, and the history of a specific part of the castle.

As we entered the hall we were met by the usual grim, oppressive atmosphere, but this time it appeared to be much more intense than I had experienced on the previous occasion. It seemed that whatever presence was in the hall did not want anybody there. Many people confessed to experiencing feelings of hostility in that room, and the group leader, who had dealt with hauntings before, claimed the atmosphere was projecting a warning. He told us he had been in similar situations, where the atmosphere felt very similar, and unpleasantness had followed. He called the group together, and advised that if anybody had second thoughts or were unsure about what lay ahead, then they had best leave now. The whole situation proved to be too much for one woman, and she bravely said her goodbyes and left the castle.

It was time to begin. We gathered around the old dining table in the center of the room and sat down, directly below the balcony that leads into the chapel. I was asked to share my previous experiences with the group and knowledge of any other supposed spirits and hauntings in the castle. Once the leader felt acquainted, he decided it was time to conduct a séance. We turned out the lights in the hall; our only means of sight was by the small flickering flame of the candle that we had borrowed from the chapel.

The leader asked us to join hands around the table. This amused my friend greatly, it was her first visit. Her light hearted attitude toward the whole situation was about to change dramatically. The séance was about to begin. The leader explained that physical contact with other sitters around the table was necessary, as entities that wished to make contact needed to use energy produced by people at the sitting, and that it provided a portal that allowed them access to our realm. The connected circle of hands supposedly increased the density of the energy at the table, creating a specific area of focus for the entity to concentrate on, like a flashlight in the dark, guiding them, to the door that leads to our plane.

Hands clasped tightly together, eyes concentrating on the flame that stood still and tall, the group listened intently for instructions. The group leader asked us to close our eyes, and bow our heads. We were instructed to take slow, deep breaths and try to empty our minds of all thoughts. He wanted us to reach a relaxed, empty state of mind, which would improve susceptibility for whatever may approach the group. He began by asking in a calm but assertive voice, "are there any spirits within the walls of this castle who would like to make contact with us? We mean you no harm. We are here to help you, to help you move on. Use the energy provided by this group of people to help make yourself known."

The silence and atmosphere in the room was eerie. It had been very similar to the grey apartment, moments before our noisy guest made its presence known. I glanced over to my brother and friend, who sent a look of grave concern back over the table. They too, knew what I was thinking.

Suddenly, the temperature in the room plummeted. It had dropped so low, that our breath was beginning to condense. Members of the group began to shiver, looking nervously around the table, as if to see if anybody else was paying attention to the change in climate. It was mid-August, and the weather outside had been warm and humid all evening. Possibly a natural occurrence, but nobody offered to leave the room and check if it had been the same outside, leaving the phenomenon open for speculation. Leaving the room to walk down the lonely, dark corridor to check the temperature outside seemed a bit challenging, considering the intensity of the atmosphere in the room. Maybe something was lurking in the dark shadows of the hallway! Nevertheless, we all had the same feelings, although nobody spoke. The expressions of worry etched on the faces of the sitters said more than words ever could.

The candle flame that stood calm and still before, began to flicker. We watched in terror as it danced and shook violently, even though there was no breeze. It grew taller, then shorter, then shook again, as though somebody had crept up close to it and blew gently at the flame. It was not possible for anybody to have achieved this from where they were sitting, as the table was six feet wide in diameter and ten feet in length. A sitter would have to have breathed heavy to have reached the flame, which would have been impossible without the sounds of exhaling breath being evident. We looked at each other in shock, as all lips remained tightly shut while the candle continued its aggressive movements.

While we watched the candle, four members of the group jolted back and shrieked as they looked at the balcony directly above us. They claimed to have seen what looked like a shadow scurry across the floor and up the stone steps before vanishing into the chapel. The four witnesses were spread apart from each other at the far side of the table with other sitters separating them, and had not met before that night, making an attempt to organise a fake ghost sighting unlikely. Furthermore, the witnesses were not facing each other directly, as they were sat down one side of the table, making signaling for simultaneous actions impossible without getting noticed. Once the shaking and terrified witnesses had been reassured, and the chapel and balcony checked for intruders, the sitting recommenced and what happened next made my blood run cold, and satisfied my belief that the castle was undoubtedly haunted, not that I needed much convincing after my previous visit.

One sitter asked the witnesses if they could describe any distinguished features of the shadow that had walked into the chapel. Unfortunately, not much else was clear, other than the fact that it had appeared to be excessively tall, over six feet with broad shoulders, resembling that of a brutishly framed man. From what I knew of the history of the castle and its historic figures, the description seemed to fit that of the infamous John Sage. He was a big man, his appearance as terrifying as his merciless mind set.

The group leader decided that an effort to draw his spirit to the séance may be possible. He explained that if the shadow the four sitters had seen was in fact the spirit of John Sage, then he was already there in the atmosphere of the room. All we had to do was summon him, and draw him nearer, down from the dark, silent chapel, across the balcony, and down the old creaking steps to where we were all sat. The thought was unbearable. However, we had come for a scare and maybe this would be the ultimate experience. After all, it would be a pity to back out now, after that long journey.

I was beginning to think the greater pity was to come, the pity that we did not leave while we had the chance. John Sage had been an evil man in life and it would be silly to think that he was incapable of inflicting misery in spirit form. The sitters were unaware of who this man had actually been, and I was beginning to feel as though it was my responsibility to share what knowledge I had of him, to at least give everyone the option to back out but while I battled with my conscience, lost in thought, I had not noticed that all my options had been removed. It was too late. The sitting had begun once more…

"John Sage, are you here? If you are here, can you give us a sign?"

Almost as soon as the group leader had finished his summons, the candle flame began to move strangely again. It started once more with its dancing, growing and shrinking before stopping abruptly, remaining still. The flame remained like this for a few seconds then it vanished. We were plunged into darkness. It was as though somebody had wet the tips of their fingers, walked over to the candle, nipped the wick and extinguished the flame. The group sat in silence, unable to comprehend what just happened. I felt my hands tighten as the sitters on my left and right squeezed with fear. I felt the hairs stand up on the back of my neck, goose bumps creeping up my arms and down my back. We were all frozen with fear. Nobody could talk. I peered into the murky darkness unable to see a thing.

The atmosphere was so oppressive I could feel my stomach churning, as though I needed to vomit. The cold in the room was almost unbearable. The sense of danger was prominent, and it was obvious that this feeling had spread around the sitters. Nobody was prepared to face whatever stood in the dark. The curious had now become reluctant to go any further, the skeptics terrified, the nervous now inconsolable, and the believers sensing that going any further was unnecessary as we had experienced enough already and it did not take a genius to work out that danger lay ahead if we were to continue. Nobody could describe why they made that assumption, it was just a general feeling that something unpleasant was about to begin.

Finally, on came a torch light. One of the sitters had made the decision on behalf of us all, and relieved the group of that bitter darkness, of which something was lurking. The sitter walked with the torch over to the light switch and flicked it on, filling the room with a calming light that we had missed so much. A sigh of relief sounded simultaneously around the room. Whatever had been in the room was there no more. The atmosphere slowly returned to a state of calm. Even though the light had returned, some sitters complained for a short while after, that they felt the presence was still there, and that we were being watched intently. It seemed as though our visitor had taken a slow walk back to the chapel, glaring at us as it climbed the steps and made its way across the balcony.

We all agreed that the séance had left us exhausted and petrified and that anymore ghostly goings on would simply be too much to handle. As we stood up from the table, eager to leave the castle, the group leader shouted "Oh wait, we haven't listened to the tape recorder yet. Maybe something was recorded during the séance!"
I swallowed hard, as I reluctantly sat down again, the other sitters cautiously taking their seats, staring at the dictaphone that lay in the center of the table. I was anxious, but curious about what may have been recorded on the tape. To this day, I wish I had never listened to it.

We sat staring at the group leader with eyes of uncertainty as he picked up the dictaphone. He explained that EVP (Electronic Voice Phenomenon) was a modern method of communication with the deceased, where eerie messages could often be discovered after a sitting. Apparently, ghosts exist in a plane that is parallel to ours, and we require a particularly high level of frequency to hear them speak, which is beyond the ability of the human ear. Tape recorders provide this frequency, allowing spirits to clearly communicate. It is suggested that animals, specifically dogs, can hear voices of the departed due to their hearing range. There have been many recorded cases where dogs have been taken to supposedly haunted houses where their behaviour and reactions have been monitored to verify a potential haunting. A dictaphone is set to record during a séance and the dog watches intently and when it shows signs of awareness, such as ears pricking up or barking, the tape recorder is stopped. After rewinding and replaying, a voice is often heard on the tape at the time the dog reacted.
The group leader looked at the anxious faces around the table and asked if anybody had any objections to playing the tape. He warned

that from his experience, some messages could be very disturbing. Taking the sitters silence as a gesture of approval, he pressed the play button. The tape began with a gentle crackling sound. Suddenly, a familiar voice joined in. It was the group leader. We heard him speak as he had throughout the séance, asking for any spirits to make themselves known. We listened as the leader's voice summoned the spirit of John Sage, along with the cries of the sitters who had seen the shadow on the balcony. Nothing unusual but a painful reminder of the fear we all felt at that particular point during the sitting.

Soon, we reached the point of the tape where the candle had been extinguished. We knew this because at the time this happened, a sitter had shouted, "what happened to the candle?" which clearly sounded on the tape, before we all sat in silence, in the dark. Although at the time the hall was quiet, the tape had a different story to tell.

After the sitter asked what had happened to the candle, there was silence for a minute or so on the tape. This was clearly the period where we had sat in the dark, terrified. Suddenly, the silence on the tape was broken by an almighty roar. It was a deep bellowing sound that boomed from the tape. All the sitters jumped back in their seats at the sheer shock of this demonic noise. Next, the shrill cries and blood curdling screams of what can only be described as men, women and children in severe pain, bounced from the tape simultaneously. The noises were so horrific that some of the sitters had to cover their ears. I winced at the sounds, my stomach knotting at every wail and shriek. The group leader dropped the tape at this point and cupped his mouth in horror. This had clearly terrified him. The cries carried on for thirty seconds or so combined with sounds of vicious growling, demonic hissing and gargling noises when suddenly, the noises stopped, leaving us with the gentle cracking of the tape once more. We all sat, staring at the dictaphone on the table, shocked and frozen with fear, as the recorder came to the end of its reel.

At this point, four members of the group stood up, and charged out the room. They didn't say a word. About a minute or so later, we heard the distant sound of a car engine as it screeched down the drive of the castle. They had gone. No goodbyes, no opinions about what they heard, they had simply stood up and ran away. And who could blame them? What we experienced was something that could easily have been depicted in a horror movie, a real life paranormal experience. That is the best way to describe the situation.

The group leader sat for a while, as we all did, in total shock, before suggesting that we all left. Nobody said anything; we just picked up our belongings and walked out the castle, a lot quicker than we had come in, got in our cars and drove away. Before entering my car, a fellow sitter had approached me and said, "We should do this again sometime" with a grin of sarcasm on his face. We appreciated his attempt to lighten the mood, but we all knew that nobody would be eager for a second attempt. If it was proof that we were after about the existence of ghosts, then we had surely got it and nobody wanted to go through that again. Many paranormal investigators or ghost hunters will confess that being scared can offer a thrill of excitement. We had all gone beyond that thrill, too far if you like, and experienced true horror.

Many years have passed since that night, and I never saw any of the sitters again. There never was a second attempt to conduct such a séance. We had experienced all we could handle of the paranormal that night. One of my friends, who had been on previous visits with me to the castle, never returned. I am no longer in contact with him, and I have my suspicions that he wanted to forget the experience so much, that the only way he could truly do so was by breaking contact with me. I guess the moral of the story is to take precautions before conducting paranormal investigations. Prepare yourself mentally for what may lie ahead, and remain open minded. The world of the supernatural has yet to be accounted for, and I think many people choose to deny its existence through fear of the unknown. Dealing with the unknown leaves no room for doubt, and people must be prepared for anything. We were clearly not prepared that evening.

The fireplace in the Minstrels Hall –the entrance to the old torture chamber

It was not until a year or so later that I made a gruesome discovery, which could possibly explain the cries recorded on tape that night.

Directly below the floor of the Minstrels hall, where the séance took place, is the original torture chamber of the castle that was used hundreds of years ago. It had been bricked up at some point during the 12th century and has remained unopened ever since. Could the heart rendering cries that had bellowed from the tape be the voices of tortured prisoners from the bloody feud days? A disturbing thought, but potentially a possibility?

The Apparition

On a visit some years later with my wife, Jemma, and friends, Jamie and Kris, I had once again, decided to stay in the Grey apartment. After hearing about the incident that took place during the séance, they were eager to see if the stories were true and although six years had passed since that fearful night, I was still convinced that the entity that prowled the gallery was still in residence. I was hoping it would entertain my wife and friends as it had done when I was sixteen.

It was 23rd December 2007. The weather was cold and bleak, as it had been six years before. The atmosphere around the apartment and castle was as intense as it has always been. I was sure that something would happen that night. I was not disappointed.

It was around midnight, and we were all set to go for a walk around the grounds. We were equipped with video camera and flashlight, ready to catch anything that jumped out of the shadows. Of course, I had never seen a ghost before, but due to previous experiences at the castle, I was not against the possibility that I might. We started down the spiral staircase that leads from the apartment down into the courtyard. The air was crisp and still, emphasising every sound. We walked across the courtyard, through the still room, down the corridor that leads to what was the old nursery, and out the side entrance, which brings you out at the small car park next to the guardroom. We walked down the gravel path towards the caretakers lodge, watching and listening carefully. I walked at the back trying to adjust the video camera to suit night conditions while Jamie and Jemma walked about twenty yards in front.

As we quietly made our way along the path, the silence was broken by the panic stricken wail of our friend Jamie. I looked up to see Jamie staring into the trees as he cautiously and very slowly made his way backwards, eyes almost bulging from their sockets. It looked as though he was carefully backing away from a lion that was getting ready to pounce in the woods. I watched as Jemma asked Jamie what the problem was. She stood next to him, trying to catch a glimpse of whatever it was that had frightened him.

Suddenly, he jumped backwards and grabbed Jemma's arm, "Jemma, run!" he shouted and before he had even finished his words, he was bolting back towards me, with Jemma close by. Expecting him to stop, I opened my mouth to ask what was wrong but as I took my breath, he sprinted past me, heading towards the side entrance of the castle. He jerked open the door and ran inside. Jemma, who was slightly shocked by Jamie's reaction, explained that he looked as though he had seen something in the woods. On looking, Jemma could not make out anything at all.

When we found him at the apartment, he was pale and shaking. We poured him a stiff drink to help him calm his nerves and after a while, he felt well enough to explain what happened.

When walking past the woods, a flash of light had caught his eyes. Upon inspection, he could see, in the distance, what looked like a robed figure. He described it as brilliant white. Suddenly, the figure disappeared and then reappeared moments later, about ten feet closer than it had been. Then it disappeared again, appearing a few seconds later another ten feet closer. By this point, Jamie could see the figure as clear as day.

It was a robed figure, wearing its hood up, obscuring the face. Its arms were folded across the chest, tucked into the sleeves of the opposite arm. It stood about five feet ten inches in height, slim built, and stood there motionless. It did not move or make a sound. It was impossible to see if it was male or female but, one thing was for sure, it was a person. Just as Jamie had caught Jemma's attention, the figure simply disappeared. He described its movements similar to that of a slide show, standing in one place one second, and then very quickly vanishing and manifesting a few feet closer.

Chillingham has a habit of producing supernatural activity that, although inexplicable at the time, produces facts and information later that can potentially verify the phenomenon. We were to discover some time later that the place where Jamie had seen the robed figure was in fact a monastery centuries ago. It had been burned down during the border wars between the English and the Scots, killing all the priests. Those who did survive were simply taken into the castle for torture, followed by execution. Could the ghostly monk that Jamie witnessed have been a priest from the monastery that had met his untimely death there? Jamie is not alone, however. Many people have reported seeing a phantom priest in the gardens at the front of the castle for decades.

If Jamie was hoping for a peaceful night of rest after his ordeal, he would be wrong. That evening we all decided to sleep in the same room and shortly after 11pm we were awoken by the sounds of what sounded like furniture being dragged around in the apartment above. Thumping, banging, scraping and crashing all night long, eventually ending at 5am, just as it had been years before. The uninvited guest had returned! The next morning, we were eager to find out if anybody had been staying in the apartment above us, and I wasn't in the slightest bit surprised to find out that it had, once again, been empty all night.

Hard Evidence?

I had become extremely curious as to what had been responsible for the unearthly pounding in the Lookout apartment at night. It was the same scenario every time we visited, year after year. Pounding, crashing, thumping and scraping, from midnight until dawn. I was determined to solve the mystery and I had come well equipped with a video camera and dictaphone.

For the first time ever, I had booked the Lookout apartment as well as the Grey, for two nights, allowing me access to the Lookout for the next forty eight hours. Whoever or whatever was responsible for the hideous noises at night, I was sure to catch. We did not plan to sleep in the Lookout, but instead set up video cameras around the apartment while we slept below in the Grey.

We had a big team that year. I was due to marry Jemma the following month, and I could not think of a better way to celebrate the end of my bachelor life than a thorough ghost hunt at Chillingham. I was accompanied by my brother Iain, and our friends, Shaun, Jamie, Kris, Bryan and Matt, most of who were believers and had previous experiences at the castle, but there were one or two skeptics. I didn't mind. It was a good mix and we had a healthy balance of open mindedness. It was a chance for the skeptics to become believers, and the believers to have the pleasure of saying I told you so!

The snow had fallen thick that day and access to the castle grounds had been almost impossible. On arrival we were informed that all other guests had cancelled due to the adverse weather conditions and we would be pretty much alone for the next two days. I was overjoyed at the news. It was an ideal situation for our investigation. The fact that we were the only people around cancelled out the possibility of pranksters, not that Chillingham needed to fake any phenomenon! If anything, it was an advantage to validating any activity that we experienced to the skeptics within our group.

Night fell at 5pm, and with it, the temperature. We peered out the bedroom window and watched the only two staff members on duty that day fight through three feet of snow to reach their lodge at the end of the drive. Now we were truly alone. Not a soul was in the castle. Not a living one anyway!

Before we settled down to bed, we had to set up the video camera in the Lookout apartment. I placed it on a table in the bedroom from where I estimated the noises to be coming from for all these years. The bedroom is directly above the bedroom in the Grey, in which we all slept. We agreed that if we all slept downstairs in the same room, then everybody could be spoken for if any activity were to take place. Even when members of the group were given the option to sleep in the bedroom next door, they declined! Safety in numbers, they said! So much for being a brave skeptic! I locked the door to the Lookout, put the key in my pocket and made my way back downstairs for the night. I was the last person to leave the room.

All was quiet until 1am. I never slept. Nobody did. The thought of the camera recording away in that lonely room seemed to send a chill down my spine. If anything was creeping around up there, it was being filmed at that moment in time. Then it began. Scraping and crashing and pounding. The ceiling vibrated as the sounds came crashing into our room. Carry on all night if you wish, I thought. The evidence will be fantastic. We all lay there listening. Nobody made a sound.

Similar experiences continued over the next two days. Nothing I wasn't used to. An amazing visit, as it always is. Once home, I unpacked the camera and began to review our recordings. I watched intently, waiting for the entity to begin its work. The room looked still, unnatural, and then it started.

The camera had picked up all the sounds we had heard in the night, however there was something different. The camera had picked up the sounds of footsteps padding around the room. The phantom footsteps, walked out the room, and into the hall. I could hear them moving back and forward as though somebody or something was pacing the apartment. Next, an eerie wind started, bellowing around the room. No windows had been open, and it had been a calm, frosty night. Through the sound of the wind whistling around the apartment I could make out what can only be described as a demonic grunt! There were several of them throughout the recorded footage. These grunts continued after the wind had stopped, and slowly faded away. The next part of the recording almost made me leap out of my skin. It sounded like heavy footsteps running out the bedroom, followed by the sounds of a door crashing shut. That was the end of the phenomenon, and nothing more appeared on the tape. I had indeed caught something, but nothing appeared and not an item of furniture moved an inch in that room. One thing was for sure, there was definitely something at work in that apartment, and it made as much noise as it liked, but managed to conceal its identity. Whatever it is must be a lot smarter than I thought.

When I showed the footage to the rest of the group, they were just as terrified as me. Kris literally jumped out of his seat after the first thump! "I think you may have something there mate" said Shaun. I took that as a major compliment, considering Shaun was almost as skeptic as they came. Footage of the haunting was one thing, but I was becoming restless. I really wanted to see this entity that made such a racket every time I tried to get some rest. Dare I sleep in that room next time I go?

Look out in the Look out!

A little over a year later, Jamie and I were back at Chillingham. We had booked the Lookout for a night, in a bid to finally catch that noisy spirit whom had caused umpteen restless nights for us over the years, while in the Grey below. Sadly, there was nothing to report during the night, but there was a very strange incident that took place late afternoon while we were relaxing in the lounge.
As we sat on the sofa, absorbing the quiet and peaceful atmosphere, which made a change from the sudden oppressive chills that would emerge when an entity was close by, we heard a noise. It sounded like the main door to the apartment had been opened. We glanced at each other as the door handle creaked, and the door glided open, or so we thought. Footsteps followed as though somebody were walking about in the hall. Convinced that it may have been the cleaner, whom we had been speaking to in the apartment earlier, and had possibly forgotten an item of equipment.

As we stood up to assist who ever had supposedly entered the apartment, the door to the lounge slowly opened. We watched in disbelief as it opened by seven inches or so, revealing nobody on the other side. Stepping back in shock, we watched as the door slowly closed again after a moment of remaining open. Footsteps began again, walking quickly back towards the apartment door.

We stood there, speechless, as we heard what sounded like the apartment door handle twist again, the door creak open and slam shut, as though somebody was leaving the apartment. I can remember not feeling particularly scared at this incident. I think the reason may have been because we were actually convinced that somebody had opened the door to the apartment and walked down the passage toward the lounge. The alarm bells did not start to ring until the door to the lounge opened stayed still for a moment then closed again, as though somebody had opened the door to see who was inside. It was also strange how no grim atmosphere accompanied the incident, which was rare in my experience of investigating paranormal activity.

After a thorough check of the apartment, nothing was found. What made the incident even stranger was when we checked the front door, it was locked. Jamie suddenly remembered that he had locked the door about an hour previously, and had the key in his pocket the whole time. Baffled, we returned to the lounge, finding it very difficult to return to our previous state of relaxation, as you could probably understand.

A Mirror Image

This incident took place without us even knowing, and it was not until a few days later that a shocking discovery would be made. I had purchased a Polaroid camera after reading that they apparently worked well for capturing apparitions.

We were staying in the Dairy apartment that year, and one of the rooms felt particularly strange. It was the last room at the end of the ground floor. A pleasant room to look at, with a wonderful interior including an old fashioned swing mirror that stood in the corner.
A blood chilling atmosphere had engulfed the room at around 11pm. It seemed strange that the rest of the apartment should feel fine except for this one room. The heating was thumping through the apartment, but this bedroom did not seem to feel the benefit of it, even though the radiator was turned on full.

It is suggested that when a room remains strangely cold, even when the heating is on full, then there could be a presence residing there. We decided to investigate further and entered the room. After a few moments of walking around failing to see anything, we decided that it would be a good idea to take a photo of the room and maybe capture a ghostly image. I noticed that I was down to my last few picture cartridges and decided that to prevent the picture from being a waste, I asked my two friends to stand next to the old mirror for the photo, that way, if no ghostly figures appeared, then I would at least have a nice photograph of my friends. After the picture jumped out the camera, we examined it. Nothing appeared to be unusual about the photo except this grey shadow that loomed in the mirror next to my friends. We thought it was probably just a lighting issue.

It was not until we arrived home a few days later that I decided to look at the photo again. This shadow seemed odd, and nothing like any other lighting issues I had had with the camera before. I decided that a closer look was in order, as the image was quite small, as is the case with most Polaroid pictures. When I glanced through the magnifying glass, I noticed that the shadow was no ordinary shadow. It was the clear form of a person, so clear that I could make it out instantly to be a World War One soldier. Through the murky grey of the shadow I could make out the image of a man wearing an old tin helmet, thick long trench coat, with a pouch hanging at his waist, connected to a long strap around his right shoulder. It is not possible to make out the age of the soldier as his face is slightly obscured, but if you look close

enough, you can make out the outline of a nose, ears, and mouth.

What makes the existence of the picture irritating is that my friends are in the photograph, which leaves its authenticity open to scrutiny. I have heard it all, "Oh you can clearly see that it is just your friends reflection," is the most common opinion. My reply is simple. If you look carefully at the photograph you will notice that there is a vase and other ornaments sitting on the cabinet just in front of the mirror, they are reflected perfectly in the mirror with colour and no obscurity. Surely if it was my friend's reflections, then they too would appear in the mirror as normally as the other objects. Secondly, I can't remember my friend wearing a tin helmet, trench coat and ammunition pouch at the time the photo was taken! Thirdly, the position that my friends took next to the mirror when the photo was taken instantly excludes them as responsible, as far as I am concerned, because they were not in a position that would show a full reflection of them in the mirror. They are stood to the side of the mirror, avoiding it. The figure that I can see looks as though it is staring out of the reflective glass, with a full frontal view.

The eerie apparition of a soldier in the mirror.

Conclusion

Most visitors to Chillingham ask when they first come, "Have you any ghosts?"

I asked the same question when I first came to the castle as a bride and in reply was told, "We do not allow them."

And very wise it was to forestall either the young guest who might play pranks, or the household whose duties might be interrupted if they began to imagine foolish things.
Chillingham should certainly afford shelter to many wraiths of its departed owners and former dwellers there.

For almost 800 years the long procession stretches, of men, women and little children who have lived, loved and suffered therein.

Leonora Tankerville   Chillingham Castle   1925

www.chillingham-castle.com
Ghosts of Chillingham castle, Richard Felix,
www.felixfilms.net, www.richardfelix.co.uk

The above passage is an extract from the diary of Leonora Tankerville, who resided at the castle during the 1920's. From her writing, I think it is clear that she believed the possibility of supernatural happenings would not be an unusual occurrence at Chillingham, giving its history, age and string of occupants throughout the centuries. If there are such things as ghosts, then there is no doubt in my mind that Chillingham meets the criteria for the status of 'haunted'.

The purpose of this book was to give you an insight into a way of life that perished long ago, and a brief history of nobility and aristocracy that is a proud part of our English heritage. Another purpose is to make you consider the possibility of the existence of ghosts, by providing a log of personal experiences and detailed descriptions of alleged hauntings at the castle that have stood the test of time for centuries.
When we consider the years of suffering, pain, and misery inflicted in such a place, is it really difficult to consider the possibility of a restless soul? Could past members of noble families have enjoyed such a life at Chillingham that they wish to stay, even after their death? From my own experience, certainly no doubt!

Whatever you choose to believe, I hope that you have enjoyed this book. If you experience anything, it will most certainly be a warm welcome by the dedicated, friendly staff and owners of Chillingham, who have provided nothing less than an outstanding and enjoyable experience throughout my years as a guest.

Included in the appendix is a guide to conducting your own paranormal investigation. Do not worry if you forget to take your ghost hunting kit to Chillingham. I am sure that the spirits that dwell there will find you eventually!

Sleep tight and have a peaceful night...

Appendix: How to conduct a paranormal investigation

•   Have the right attitude.

Many people set unrealistic expectations when attending a ghost hunt. Very few people actually 'see' an apparition. Hauntings come in many forms, some of which are included in the 'personal experiences' section of this book, such as noises and change in atmosphere or mood in a particular place. Don't expect too much. Doing so may diminish your ability to notice the smallest of phenomena, such as a gentle padding of ghostly footsteps!

•   Have the right equipment.

Ghost hunters do not need top of the range equipment to gather evidence. A simple digital camera or Polaroid will capture an entity if it is there. Be sure to choose a camera with a flash, as a darkened room will be difficult to make out on a photograph. A tape recorder is always useful, as EVP can appear without you even noticing; therefore it may be useful to keep the recorder running at all times, taking it with you everywhere you go.

•   Do not take chances with things you do not understand.

As you may have gathered from this book, some entities can be quite malevolent and capable of activity that you may not expect. Always consider the possibility that harm may be possible, and use your judgment to decide when it is time to end a séance or hunt. The consequences, particularly emotionally, can be quite severe, especially for the faint hearted.

•   Don't go alone.

As the saying goes, safety in numbers! If you are investigating a particularly old building, there may well be rooms that are unsafe due to neglect and lack of repair through time. Loose bricks or floor cavities could cause serious injury to the individual. It is advisable to investigate in groups of no less than three people, therefore somebody is on hand to treat any injuries instantly or call for assistance. You may also wish to pack a first aid kit and mobile phone, just in case. In the paranormal sense, you may encounter something unpleasant, and nobody would like to be alone in that situation!

- Be patient.

Even the most haunted of locations have periods of time where activity may lay dormant. You must remember that something will happen eventually, and staying aware will help a great deal. If nothing happens, which there is always a possibility, don't be disheartened and don't give up! You may find when you return to the location at a later date, you will be in for a surprise. Always expect the unexpected!

- Enjoy!

About the Author

Mark Fisher lives with his wife Jemma, in South Shields. He graduated from Durham University with a degree in education and also achieved Qualified Teacher Status. He currently works in the Education sector.

Printed in Great Britain
by Amazon

21823903R00030